THE SHORT AND BLOODY HISTORY OF HIGHWAYMEN

THE SHORT AND BLOODY HISTORY OF HIGHWAYMEN

John Farman

Lerner Publications Company/Minneapolis

13170303

This book is available in two editions:
Library binding by Lerner Publications Company, a division of Lerner Publishing Group
Soft cover by First Avenue Editions, an imprint of Lerner Publishing Group
241 First Avenue North
Minneapolis, MN 55401 U.S.A.

Website address: www.lernerbooks.com

Map on page 37 by Tim Seeley.

Library of Congress Cataloging-in-Publication Data

Farman, John
    The short and bloody history of highwaymen / by John
Farman—1st American ed.
        p.   cm.
    Includes index.
    Summary: Presents a detailed account of the daily life of
highwaymen, and introduces some of the famous men and women
who earned their living as robbers in Great Britain in the eighteenth
century.
    ISBN: 0-8225-0839-7 (lib. bdg. : alk. paper)
    ISBN: 0-8225-0840-0 (pbk. : alk. paper)
    I. Brigands and robbers—Great Britain—History—Juvenile
literature. 2. Brigands and robbers—Great Britain—Biography—
Juvenile literature. [1. Robbers and outlaws—Great Britain.] I. Title.
HV6453.G7 F37 2002
364.15'52'0941—dc21   2001050689

Manufactured in the United States of America
1 2 3 4 5 6 – JR – 07 06 05 04 03 02

CONTENTS

WHO, WHAT, AND WHERE
WERE HIGHWAYMEN?

It's a dark, moonless night about 300 years ago. There you are, riding home from the theater, minding your own business, when out of the shadows comes a lone rider with a small mask and a large pistol demanding your money or your life. What sort of a guy would do that? Is he just a land-based pirate? I sincerely hope you want to know.

Pirates à la Mode

Highwaymen were very different from pirates. Okay, when push comes to shove, they did practically the same thing as pirates—rob people. But, they did it on a horse rather than in a boat. Much more interesting, I think, is the fact that many of the highwaymen were gentlemen who came from distinguished backgrounds. And, even if they weren't, they certainly acted like they were (if you see what I mean).

Plenty of these highway robbers grew up in wealthy homes and received proper upbringings (like your dear selves). Despite these early advantages, most of them saw their lives turn sour at some stage. Some were kicked out of the family home for inappropriate behavior, while others were left out of a will after the death of a rich daddy or uncle. William Parsons, for instance, had a father who was a baronet (a rank below baron and above knight) and an aunt who was a duchess. Poor Bill went to Eton (a very exclusive boys' school), was expelled, gambled away his fortune, took to the road, and ended his illustrious career swinging from the gallows at Tyburn in central London. As far as we know, he was the only ex-Etonian to go into the highway robbery business.

Blown the Lot

Others received their inheritance but simply blew the whole caboodle in a feast of loose living or lost it at the many English gambling establishments of the 1700 and 1800s. So, what really connected them was that they were all broke, overdrawn, bankrupt, penniless, or whatever you want to call it and faced the terrifying prospect of having to earn an honest living like everyone else. They couldn't even claim social injustice as an excuse.

These guys wouldn't dare to be seen working real jobs (like you and me*). So in order to live in the style to which they'd become accustomed, robbing those people who'd managed to hang onto their wealth was the only avenue open to them.

COSTLY LIFESTYLE TO SUPPORT

How?

Simple! They owed it to the roads—or, should I say, the lack of roads. Practically no one had built any roads since the brilliant Romans visited England some 1,200 years before. These days, we take roads for granted. We steer the car or bike out of the driveway onto a neatly paved street and easily get wherever we want to go on similar interconnecting roads and highways. But travel wasn't always so easy.

Just imagine, the eighteenth-century equivalents of our freeways were nothing more than broad tracks through fields.

---

* *Writing this stuff is a real job—who am I kidding?*

They became almost impassable in the sopping wet, muddy winters and almost as impassable in the summers when the deep ruts baked hard like overdone pizzas.

Not only that, the population of England in the seventeenth century only numbered around six million. Thus wide expanses of deserted forests and public land offered just a few well-worn tracks to follow. Very few houses existed along these roads—never mind the abundant service stations we have in modern times. Travelers over 200 years ago could plod along for hours and hours on end without passing any sign of another living soul. Add to that no street lighting and that the coaches moved at a snail's pace (fast snails admittedly) and often broke down at the drop of an axle, and you have the perfect hunting ground for the notorious "gentlemen of the road."

Others

Of course, other sorts of men became highwaymen. Many served as soldiers during the English civil war (1642–1649). When the armies were disbanded, they found themselves at the point of starvation, miles from home, and without any prospect of earning an honest day's wages. The real peak of soldiers entering the highwaymen "profession" occurred between 1697 and 1701, when a bunch of unemployed, disillusioned, and thoroughly desperate soldiers returned from the wars with France.

Other highwaymen held perfectly respectable jobs but used them as a cover for their nighttime activities. William Davis, a landholder born in northern Wales, for instance, was called the "Golden Farmer" because nobody could understand how he became so rich from farming. Likewise John Cottington cleaned chimneys by day and was a robber by night (at least he saved himself the trouble of having to blacken up for camouflage!).

By the Way

Many of the would-be high-waymen actually rented their first horse rather than risk being caught aboard a stolen animal.

How Often?

Don't think, like I did, that robberies by highwaymen were relatively few and far between. On the contrary, it appears that it was rare *not* to be bushwhacked, or at least chased and threatened, if you journeyed any great distance across England during the golden age of highwaymen (1700–1800). As one much-robbed and weary traveler put it, "highwaymen are as common as crows." As for crossing London, many wealthy gentlefolk employed a special servant (often armed) to

accompany them and hopefully discourage the footpads (unmounted robbers) who seemed to lurk in every alleyway and behind every tree.

What's Coming?

So, get ready for descriptions of the illegal comings and goings of famous and not-so-famous highwaymen (and highway-women). In addition, and this is much more fun, I'll let you in on what it was actually like to be one—on a day-to-day basis: the upside and, much more to the point, the downside of life as a lone robber on the open highways and byways of England.

BUTCHERS UNITE

If you looked through the records of highwaymen executions at Tyburn, you'd notice that there seem to be more ex-butchers than any other profession who were hanged as highwaymen. This may seem a bit weird at first. I mean, can you see the connection between meat and highway robbery (apart from the expense)?

At the end of the seventeenth century, butchers saw themselves as a cut* above the commoners and were considered respectable professionals (not to mention well-off). But, as the century wore on, the ordinary butcher lost this reputation and started to associate with the more criminal elements (like some used-car salesmen these days).

So why did butchers become highwaymen? For a start, being in the dead animal business, so to speak, made butchers very aware of meat's value. The beasts often traveled to and from the countryside like walking cash. In fact, meat in its various living forms either waddled, plodded, shuffled, or skipped its way along every muddy road into London (to meet its maker).

* *Bad joke!*

More to the point, the animals' owners always returned the same way, having swapped their beastly charges for hard, jingly cash.

Big Business

Meat, by the way, was a staple of the British diet in those days. The amount and quality that a man could put on his family's table indicated his economic success. In other words, meat was a status symbol. Hardly anyone grew vegetables then, unless desperately poor. In fact, anything that came out of the  ground (except bread) wasn't really regarded as real food. Meat became the biggest business around and was traded at noisy, smokey taverns. These establishments—like The Rose and Crown, The Swan with Two Necks, The Bear and Ragged Staff, or The Golden Lion—huddled around the ancient Smithfield meat market in the center of London.

It would not be going too far to say that the meat industry became the hub around which all commerce revolved. It influenced the amount of forestland cut down to provide pasture (like major fast-food chains do now to provide burgers). It affected the number of tollgates set up to maintain the hoof-trashed roads. And of course, the meat trade provided an enormous source of employment in a country consisting of mostly agricultural land.

The meat business, however, had turned corrupt by the early 1700s. Soon subquality, sometimes dangerously "off," cuts were sold on the unregulated and often criminal market by unscrupulous "jobbers." It got so bad that a lot of the respectable butchers and poulterers (and all the little businesses that relied on them) really began to feel the pinch.

Wits' End

As mostly middle-aged husbands and fathers, butchers dreaded losing their families and their homes. At their wits' end, many of these men were forced to look for other ways of making money when their trade went belly up. It didn't take them long to realize that a little highway robbery would help to restock their ailing businesses. Their inside knowledge of how the meat business worked (and how and when the cash moved around) led them to their prey. For instance, James Dalton, an ex-master butcher fallen on hard times, was caught and convicted of highway robbery three times, three times transported (sent overseas to serve time in a prison), and three times returned to London, before being hanged (one time!) in 1730. Then there's the most famous highwayman of all, Dick Turpin, who was apprenticed as a butcher and even opened his own shop before he launched into his new, much more profitable career.

All Together

And not only the butchers suffered. All the little people who surrounded the meat trade—the small-time dealers in herbs, eggs, poultry, and butter—fell on hard times as well. They actually encouraged the highwaymen to go about their criminal business. Innkeepers (called bluffers by the highwaymen) got in on the act, too. They kept a sneaky eye on the cattle drivers and cattle grazers returning from the market, especially those who carried lots of lovely gold and silver. Friends of the highwaymen gladly gave them the nod now and then.

Daniel Defoe, a famous writer of the time (*Robinson Crusoe, Moll Flanders,* etc.), cautioned travelers to keep their distance from the innkeepers or stable keepers and to be careful about how much they said to strangers, either in the inns or on the road. Even the gatekeepers were caught between loyalty to their old friends (the highwaymen) and the law that breathed down their necks.

Not the Worst Baddies

Finally, it must be said that the common folk regarded highway robbery as almost respectable. Most people saw it as the most romantic and exciting way of committing a crime. Let's face it, if you were poor, the robbing of rich people in rich coaches meant nothing to you. If anything, highwaymen were thought of as Robin Hood-like characters. Instead of receiving the public's hatred (like pirates did), they became the public's heroic figures. Everyone (even those who got robbed) enjoyed swapping stories about the highwaymen's lives and dastardly doings. Being recognized as a highwayman brought very little shame in the late seventeenth and early eighteenth centuries.

DINNERTIME IN HIGHWAYMAN-LAND

On the whole, highwaymen were lonely guys (just like writers) and were usually as solitary off duty as when they were at work. Because they were almost always hiding from the law, they only carried the possessions they could fit on the backside of a horse. Consequently, few highwaymen had real homes and real wives to go to, so most slept where they could. They lodged in inns and taverns. For food, they ordered a delivery or patronized the various cookhouses (buildings for cooking) that thrived in England during the seventeenth and eighteenth centuries. Highwaymen, by the way, gained popularity with the more dishonest owners of the taverns and cookhouses, as they often paid generously with their ill-gotten loot.

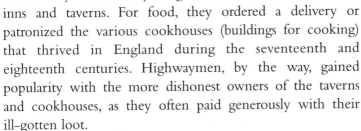

By the Way

In the eighteenth century, London employed more than 35,000 people in its eating and drinking establishments (the population as a whole still hadn't reached a million). Why the popularity, you ask? Food service was one of the only trades into which those born poor could enter with a chance of bettering themselves.

Thieves' Kitchens

In a pinch, an off-duty highwayman needing to sell some hot gear could visit the local thieves' kitchen. These secret establishments catered to all the local lowlife. The quality of the food and drink bore a great resemblance to the clientele—rough and extremely tasteless. Most of the self-respecting "gentlemen of the road" saw themselves as a cut above that sort of thing and wouldn't dream of associating with the likes of common burglars (lowly thieves were called lowpads) and pickpockets (more commonly called cutpurses in those days). Highwaymen were regarded as the elite of the underworld and only utilized these kitchens in dire situations. Luckily, they didn't often need them, as most highwaymen lived in or around London, so finding stuff to eat really late in the evening was no problem.

Restaurants

Restaurants were, as you can probably guess, a French idea (hence the French word). But in eighteenth-century England, hardly any restaurants resembled those we know today (with long menus and snooty waiters). Everyday eating houses in England seldom offered a choice of food (just like your mom doesn't). Indeed, the choice for diners eating out consisted of the meal of the day—called "the ordinary"—like it or not (again, just like home).

London and some of the bigger English cities presented streets full of cookhouses, each cooking up something slightly different. These rough-and-ready, family-run establishments mostly catered for people whose humble lodgings★ had no facilities for home cooking. The alternative was for the residents of the poorer houses to put their meals in the nearest baker's always-hot oven for a nominal fee. (This service existed well into the twentieth century in some poorer areas.)

By the Way

It's thought that the term "cockney" (referring to the natives or the dialect of the East End of London) came from the people who owned and ran the thousands of London cookhouses.

Takeout

Don't go thinking that takeout food is a new idea. All the cookhouses did a takeout service even in those days—they had to. Eating out, or simply buying your meals out, was more of a necessity than a luxury if you were less than rich. Even a highwayman might send a boy out for something to eat when he got home cold and tired after an especially hard night of robbing.

Alternatively, once he'd parked, fed, and tucked in his horse, he could buy something off the street from the many street vendors. Normal takeout featured stuff like eels, oysters, pies (or oyster pies), black puddings, cakes, and penny custards. Mmmm.

★ *Most people rented in those days.*

How Much?

In upscale places (where the better-off people went), the average price for a good meal cost around five shillings. That might seem like a bargain, but it translates into around $25 in today's money—not cheap in a society where most of the people lived on practically nothing. The more down-to-earth establishments charged far less.

In the cookhouses, the actual cooking happened in the same room as you ate. The rooms were noisy, steamy, and smokey, and there was a large piece of dead animal turning relentlessly on a spit at one end. The rotisserie was powered by a child or a dog of the family running in a treadmill on the wall. The poor pooch (known as the turnspit dog) rarely stopped and had to relieve himself as he ran (pee while you work). Health and safety regulations? I don't think so.

Also in the room was a big cauldron bubbling above the fire that contained a sort of never-ending stew. Every now and again, semiedible objects of a very dubious nature were tossed into it. Vegetables, which had for centuries been the staple diet of the poor, were rather unfashionable at that time (because they had been the staple diet of the poor). Many who could not afford much meat, however, still ate a sort of porridge, made of peas, to fill them up.

How Offal

Nothing was wasted. People in those days often ate parts of animals that we wouldn't go near, let alone eat! Grisly stuff like calf's head and feet; umble pie made from the "umbles" (guts) of venison; sheep's head and feet; ling's fin (a sort of fish); tripe (sheep's stomach); cow's udder; and ox's cheeks. And—just to make you really sick—a real delicacy was a boiled stew of all of those nasty lips and ears and noses (and much worse!*) that we throw away (or put in hot dogs or dog food). Apologies if you're squeamish (or a vegetarian).

Care for a Drink?

Highwaymen never drank water (they called it Adam's ale) when back in the city. Actually, nobody did in those days. The reason was simple—it was filthy to the point of being poisonous (as expected of water taken from a river that all the sewage flowed into). Nor did they drink cow's milk (which was called yarum), because they thought it also was unsafe,

---

* *Use your imagination.*

which it probably was. Oddly enough, donkey's milk was popular for the sick or for young children. Female donkeys were dragged around the streets of the bigger cities and milked on the spot.

Beer for All

The truth is, everyone drank beer—moms, dads, grannies, maiden aunts, clergymen—even schoolkids. In fact, the boys at Eton, the most fashionable school, were punished if they didn't drink their daily allowance (try me, try me!). There was "small" beer, which was fairly weak and "strong" beer, which most certainly wasn't—and it was all very cheap.

As for highwaymen, most of them loved to drink. Those who did were called bingo-boys (bingo meaning brandy) and they loved the places where strong drink was served. The highwaymen's very rude drinking songs made them famous. Some tunes made fun of thieves and constables, some celebrated the love of women, some were about the meat trade, some were about the exploits of fellow highwaymen and their love of the open road. Their most favorite drinking song went like this:

Now we are arriv'd to the Boozing-Ken [maybe an Inn],
And our Pockets full of Cole [money?];
We pass for the best of Gentlemen,
When over a flowing Bowl
Our Hearts are at ease,
We kiss who we please;
On Death it's a Folly to think;
May he hang in a Noose,
That this Health will refuse,
Which I am now going to drink.

Highwaymen awaiting trial in London's Newgate prison, like in many other prisons, were usually not short of hard "rhino" (the underworld term for money). They could buy liquor whenever they wanted from the jailer (who usually had a degree in corruption). There was a deadly drink called "South Sea" and a wicked gin that was made on the premises, called at various times "Cock-my-Cap," "Kill Grief," "Meat and Drink," or simply "Comfort." It sounds like the prisoners wanted an escape from their reality.

WHAT TO WEAR?

One of the highwaymen's (or highwaywomen's) greatest problems was deciding what to wear when working. Obviously, he couldn't put on his everyday clothes (called duds even then), or he'd be recognized right away. He certainly couldn't wear anything too flashy or brightly colored, or he'd attract attention while lurking in the gloom. And he couldn't wear what he wore for "work" when he came home in the morning. So what was he supposed to do?

In the late seventeenth and eighteenth century, highway robbers had a uniform. It consisted of a full-length, black embroidered jacket, a silk vest, tight buckskin breeches, a white shirt with a scarf at the neck, and black leather shoes with big shiny buckles or tall leather boots with brown fold-over tops. This was the outfit of an extremely wealthy country gentleman, in fact. On his head, the highwayman wore the obligatory three-cornered hat edged with gold braid. Underneath the hat (called a nab), he donned a girly powdered periwig tied at the back with a girly bow (which wasn't girly then). He owned lots of these wigs, each a different color from his own hair, of course. The use of false beards as part of the disguise goes without saying. Some highwaymen stuffed the ends of their wigs into their mouths to help hide their appearance. Most important, he wore a black mask over his eyes and sometimes a silk hankie over his mouth. He couldn't take any chances.

What to Wear?

Some highwaymen, like the infamous Gamaliel Ratsey (great name!) who was hanged in 1605, wore a nasty-looking hood with a nasty-looking face painted on it, covering his own nasty-looking face.

Did You Know

That the saying "to pull the wool over someone's eyes" dates from this period? As wealthy men of the period wore woolen wigs, highwaymen often pulled a victim's wig over his eyes so that he couldn't see who was robbing him.

Men as Women

Then there were the disguises. For instance, James Collett did his robbing dressed as a bishop, with his partners in crime dressed as his chaplain and servers. Perhaps more common were a number of cross-dressers. Thomas Sympson passed as an acceptable woman—too easily as it happens.

On one occasion, West Country highwayman Sympson rode in a coach with a well-known member of the noble class. He was looking so fetching that the nobleman made a pass at him (an occupational hazard). Our Tom (no doubt in his highest voice) said that he would prefer to spend some time alone with his lordship and led him away from the other passengers. Walking through the woods, the nobleman noticed that this gorgeous damsel

(later known as "Old Mob") was wearing a pair of men's pants. Women never wore pants (called kicks) in those days, so the nobleman asked Tom about her outfit. The highwayman replied that the kicks were meant to hold all of his lordship's money. He then proceeded to hold him up.

By the Way

Sympson later robbed Judge Jeffreys, the notorious hanging judge and one-time Lord Chief Justice of England. This wasn't a good career move, as Sympson ended his days in 1691 at Tyburn's gallows in front of his adoring but heartbroken wife, five kids, and countless grandchildren.

Women as Men

There were a few highwaywomen. They mostly dressed as men. Wearing men's clothes made it easier to ride horses (no skirts involved) and to cover their identity when they slipped back into their normal lives. The most famous highwaywoman, Mary Frith, was born around 1584. To be honest, she seemed manly from the beginning. I mean, how many women do you know who have a violent temper, carry a sword, smoke a pipe, and drink themselves silly every night in lowly taverns? Your mom! Oh dear, I hope I haven't put my foot in my mouth.

Moll Cutpurse

A shoemaker's daughter, Mary started out as a simple pickpocket and purse-snatcher in and around the streets of London. Throughout the teeming underworld, people called her Moll Cutpurse. She was even branded on the hand with a red-hot iron—a popular way of marking small-time thieves in those days. At sixty she decided to go into the big time. So Moll went out on the open road as a highwaywoman during the English civil war. She had loads of fun robbing the Roundheads (supporters of the British Parliament, who were opposing the king) with her friends such as the Royalist captain, James Hind.

Mary realized that the fences (receivers of and dealers in stolen goods) gave her and other thieves much less than the value of their goods. (FYI, one of these dealers was called a fencing-cully by the highwaymen, a cully being someone who is easily tricked. Those sarcastic highwaymen!) Anyway, Mary wisely decided to go into the receiving business herself. She soon became one of the biggest receivers of stolen goods and made a fortune. She eventually lived in a massive house with lots of servants, had loads of lovers, and lined her mansion wall-to-wall with mirrors.

WHO IS THE FAIREST IN THE LAND?

But bad old Mary couldn't give up "the road." She was eventually caught, tried, and sentenced to death. By that time, as you can imagine, she was so rich that she spent a massive fortune (about $185,000 in modern money) to buy a pardon. It seems outrageous that if you had enough money in olden times, you could get yourself out of practically anything.★ "He cannot be hung who hath Five Hundred Pounds at his command," wrote highwayman Francis Jackson. Mary helped prove it.

★ *That's something only politicians seem to be able to do these days.*

By the Way

Mary obviously had a great sense of the ridiculous—even near the end. She requested, while on her deathbed at the age of seventy-five, that she be buried upside down so that she could appear as preposterous in the afterlife as she had in the first one. My kind of woman.

Naked Robbery

There was one highwayman who didn't worry about clothes—he simply didn't wear any. One of the famous Cherhill gang, who terrorized Bath Road, used to leap out on his unsuspecting victims completely naked, while waving a gun and everything else (presumably). Apparently it scared them into parting with all they had on them.

TRAVELERS' TRICKS

In the 1700s, as robbery on the king's or queen's highways reached fever pitch, the travelers began to figure out the situation and developed smart ways to avoid losing their money or their lives.

Armed and Dangerous

The market for little flintlock pistols grew in the seventeenth century. They were small enough to be hidden in a pocket of a joseph (coat) or in the small muff that ladies often used to keep their hands warm. The size of the pistols meant that the firing mechanism was always on the outside, and the things could easily go off at a mere sneeze. Talk about shooting yourself in the foot!

Half Robbed

Some travelers tried to keep their not-very-hard-earned money by cutting their banknotes in two. They carried half with them and sent the rest later. Then they simply stuck the

two parts together at a later date. This stunt often miffed the highwayman so much that he shot the clever person dead—out of spite. This reaction sort of ruined the point of the exercise.

All I've Got

Most people tried the oldest trick in the book, carrying a small amount of money in an obvious place and hiding the rest in a less obvious place. The highwaymen, however, weren't stupid. They threatened to scuff up the victim (especially those that looked rich) if they found any more hidden loot. Others had their suits or dresses made with hidden pockets, or they used specially designed foot warmers with extra pockets for money and jewelery (called lurries by the highwaymen).

Home-Sewn

The women who sewed coins into the very linings of their clothes showed the most ingenuity. However, if the highwayman got wind of this scheme, he was likely to take the whole dress and leave the ladies somewhat embarrassed (not to mention chilly).

Not a Sniff

In another good trick, travelers hid valuables in something that smelled foul, like overripe cheeses (called caffin) or pungent ointments (or old socks). This worked if the travelers could put up with the smell for the whole journey.

Shooting Back

The smartest of the travelers journeyed with armed guards. Many wealthy people chose their servants according to how well they used a gun or a sword. It was not uncommon, therefore, to have a shoot-out on the journey, especially if there was a whole gang of robbers involved.

Protection Money

Some highwaymen found a way of earning money without even leaving the local tavern. Regular travelers paid them regular money NOT to be robbed when out and about. That's not all! The villains then ensured that nobody else robbed their "patrons" while they were on the highwayman's particular territory—a kind of early protection racket.

There was one superbold villain called Whitney, the self-proclaimed "King of the Highwaymen." He presented a proposal to the British government in which he offered to keep the roads clear of his fellow felons for a huge sum of money per year. The members of the government naturally declined his kind suggestion.

Not Well Pleased

Although the more refined highwaymen showed little violence toward their victims, others really lost it, especially if they smelled a cheater. These violent highway robbers had generally started their criminal careers as common footpads (street muggers) and came from a different class than the gentlemen of the road.

For a start, the worst type of highwayman used language that was less than polite. They often flung terrible insults, most of them unprintable, like: "You suffocated dogs in doublets" or "You spawn of hell hatched by Beelzebub." (These are just the nice ones!)

One unpleasant character, Patrick Fleming of Ireland, was accused of having murdered five men, two women, and a fourteen-year-old boy. He even cut off the ears, nose, and lips of a man who'd had the nerve to resist him.

There was also a particularly unpleasant character called Jacob Halsey who, among a string of dreadful things, knocked down a church usher, who fought back spiritedly. Jacob reportedly shouted, "I see you canst exercise thy long-staff [a tall pole used as a weapon] pretty well, but I'll prevent you from using your short one tonight." With that, he nailed the poor guy to a tree by his nether portion! (Ouch!!)

Andrew Baynes stripped the victims who claimed to have nothing on them. He then thrashed them with his riding crop if he found they'd been hiding anything. On one occasion, while being robbed by the vicious highwayman, a woman swallowed a very valuable ring, presumably with the idea of retrieving it later (if you get my meaning). He became angry and immediately slit her open, retrieved the ring, filled the poor woman's tummy with stones, and left her dead by the roadside.

Another, John Withers, forgot to put his mask on one day (silly chap) while robbing a postman. To avoid an embarrassing encounter at a later date, he cut the poor man's throat, sliced open his stomach, filled him (also) with stones, and chucked him into a river.

On another occasion, a woman struggled to remove her diamond wedding ring while being held up by the impatient brute. The poor dear ended up losing her finger as well.

Gilder Roy, a Scot from a very fine family, got the most pleasure from killing those who put up the least fight (unfair or what?). He once held up a judge who didn't want to part with the jewels he carried. This annoyed Gilder in a big way. He stripped the coachmen and footmen, tied them up tight, and threw them into a pond. He then hacked the coach to pieces, shot the horses (shame!), and hanged the old judge for good measure (shame, shame!).

The Royal Mail

In the olden days, many valuables moved around England by ordinary mail. With no railways or planes, everything had to go by road. Even cash traveled with the mailman. In the seventeenth and eighteenth centuries, a single rider on a single horse carried the mail throughout the country. These brave post boys rode between the inns that acted as depots for the mail.

A single man on a lonely stretch of road (inns usually sat about ten miles apart) was a sitting target for highwaymen.

The problem became so bad that huge rewards were offered to anyone who could track down the highwaymen.

The post office, founded in England in 1649, tried everything to keep the mail safe. At one point the safety measures included strong metal boxes and fully armored coaches. Right up to the end of the eighteenth century, nothing proved robber proof. The post office officials had no choice but to put their hands even deeper in their pockets. The money purchased a series of new superfast mail coaches smothered in expensive royal logos and drawn by four superhealthy horses. The driver and guard sat alone on the mailbox armed with a big gun called a blunderbuss. This nasty weapon shot a lot of little lead balls in a wide arc, which meant that the shooter didn't have to be accurate.

The new coaches tore around the country, free from toll charges. The driver blew a long post horn to warn the guards to open the tollgates as they approached. Never having to slow down gave these coaches a big advantage. Few of these coaches were ever successfully robbed.

By the Way

The tollhouses, where people paid to use a road, often held large amounts of money when the road had been particularly busy. They soon became a favorite source of loot for the highwayman. The penalty for any interference with the tollhouses was death by hanging.

REASONS TO BE WARY

Going down to the woods in the seventeenth or eighteenth century guaranteed a big surprise. English forests proved especially dangerous for travelers long ago. Also, the terrible condition of the roads greatly determined the speed at which coaches could travel (and the ease with which the highwayman could stop them).

A large percentage of highwaymen chose to live in or around London for fairly persuasive reasons. First, by far the biggest city in England, London made it easy to get lost among the throng of people who practically lived on the streets in the 1700s. Second, London turned into countryside and woodlands the moment you left the city (no suburbs in those days). Third, because there were no real banks, big money tended to move in and out of the city by road, often in the form of gold and silver. Last, the valuable stuff that wasn't gold or silver needed getting rid of (or fencing).

London offered a network of Faginlike fences. (The word "Fagin" comes from the name of a character in Charles Dickens's *Oliver Twist*. Fagin is an evil fence who presides over and corrupts a gang of young thieves.) These faceless men and their poor misguided entourage could convert anything that wasn't cash . . . into cash.

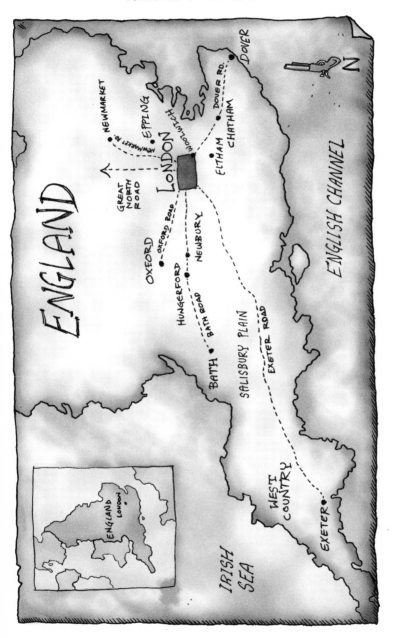

Going into or out of London gave everyone reason to be wary. The roads were bad. If you carried a lot of money, they were worse. Traveling along some particular roads became like putting your head in a lion's mouth and hoping for the best. The following roads were a magnet for highwaymen.

The Dover Road

The hilly road that ran from the port of Dover to London became dependably risky, to say the least, back in the early 1500s. Robbers favored an area near Chatham—from where the freshly paid sailors set off for London to spend their hard-earned cash. Shooters Hill in Woolwich, also on the Dover Road but nearer London, was also treacherous—hence the name. In 1797 a post chaise (a type of carriage) carrying a couple of lawyers and a midshipman from the HMS *Venerable* was stopped on Shooters Hill. The attackers severely beat the passengers and forced pistols into their mouths. The poor sailor lost all his clothes when they stole his trunk.

By the Way

Highwaymen always attacked on hills (upward) because their victims had to travel far more slowly.

The Bull Inn on Shooters Hill (particularly steep and dangerous) was a famous rest stop in those days and the first mail drop-off spot on the road out of London. Here highwaymen lurked to see who was going where and when and, more important, with what. Along Eltham Road, which crossed the Dover Road, stood a line of gibbets (places to hang people after they'd already hanged). Samuel Pepys noted in his famous diary that, in 1661 on his way to Dover, he "traveled right under the man that hangs upon Shooters Hill, and a filthy sight it is to see how the flesh is shrunk on his bones."

By the Way

Coach drivers often suffered from drowsiness caused by the rocking motion of the vehicle and the amount they drank at the coach houses. It was not unusual for a highwayman to leap out and be practically run down by the galloping horses (called prances) whose driver had fallen fast asleep.

The Bath Road

Despite Bath's reputation as an elegant and genteel city, there was nothing elegant and genteel about the road you had to take to get there. Anxious brigands (bandits) plagued the road. They eagerly robbed the wealthy travelers on their way to the famous mineral waters of Bath. An ad in the *London Gazette* of December 1, 1681, offered a reward plus expenses for information leading to the arrest of the highwaymen who held up Mr. Joseph Bullock on the section of the road between Hungerford and Newbury. The ad listed the insignificant goods stolen from Mr. Bullock and, at the end, casually mentioned the murder of his servant, John Thomas, as if it were little more than an inconvenience (which Joseph probably considered it).

Hounslow Heath

The Bath Road crossed the notorious Hounslow Heath (now part of western Greater London), which crawled with highwaymen. The heath was also crossed by the Exeter Road. This prime crossroad attracted villains, like the notorious French villain Claude Duval, looking for rich pickings. A local highwayman called Twysden frequented the area and, as legend has it, turned out to be the bishop of Raphoe in Donegal. He was shot dead while at work on Hounslow Heath. (The Lord works in mysterious ways.)

Another lord, the fifth earl of Berkeley, had a massive stately pile at Hounslow and was robbed so many times that he used to go everywhere armed to the grinders (teeth). He killed quite a few highwaymen in his time, including Cran Jones who he burned to a cinder. His clothes were set alight by one of the earl's better close-range shots.

The Great North Road

You can truly link only one man with the great North Road—Dick Turpin. He carried out innumerable robberies in the Finchley area, which later became a gloomy suburb of Greater London. Finchley Common, another favorite hanging location, was risky until well into the 1800s.

The Oxford Road

These days, on the road going north-westish out of London toward Oxford, the countryside starts around Hillingdon. In the seventeenth century, journeys began to get a bit safer near Hillingdon, because it was too far away for the highwaymen to travel to. But the bad lads usually waited at Shotover Hill, Oxford, to jump out on travelers who had almost made it.

The West Country

I don't know about you, but I still wouldn't feel that safe crossing Salisbury Plain (where Stonehenge is) at night on a horse (army patrols and druids). In the eighteenth century, it ranked up there with the stupidest thing you could do. Even farther west was the West Country (a large area in southwestern England that includes the counties of Cornwall, Devon, Exeter, and Dorset), which had always been a favorite haunt for highwaymen.

Knightsbridge

Practically the worst thing that can happen to you these days in Kensington in central London is to be accosted by some old lady asking the way to the department store Harrods or being solicited for change for a parking meter. In the 1700s, the worst thing was much worse.

Coaches often got stuck in the mud caused by the streams that then ran through Hyde Park. Right up to 1798, highwaymen hung around Knightsbridge, robbing the stranded travelers. It got so bad for a time that they needed to organize a carpool. A bell rang at intervals on Sunday evenings, like the boarding horn of a ship. It attracted people returning to London who didn't want, or dare, to travel alone. The groups of travelers only set off when they had a sufficient number to dissuade the robbers.

North out of London

The Newmarket Road going north out of London became so

dangerous that, in 1617, a hand-to-hand battle ensued between highwaymen and irate locals. They injured five of the crooks and killed at least one. Nearer to London, a bunch of recently exed soldiers, desperate to find something to do, formed a sort of highwayman's cooperative in Epping Forest. They became so successful that in the end the Lord Chief Justice was forced to send a detachment of dragoons (heavily armed troops) to "ask" the highwaymen (not very nicely) to desist. The co-op, however, only scattered and reformed elsewhere.

Did You Know?

One of the reasons the British drive on the left-hand side of the road dates back to these times. A coach driver, usually right-handed, preferred his assailant to approach on his right side. Either driving a carriage or on horseback, the driver would have his sword-arm nearest. Highwaymen, of course, soon realized this and would lurk on the nearside—out of range of a flailing blade.

TRADE SECRETS

I don't suppose that knowing how to spot highwaymen really holds much interest these days. I mean, some shady guy wearing a three-cornered hat and a mask, waiting on horseback at the corner of your street, might seem just a little obvious. But in the mid-eighteenth century, highwaymen were much more difficult to spot.

Francis Jackson (alias Dixie the Highwayman) was the first in a long line of English highwaymen who sold their stories to entertain the public. Not only that, but when he quit the biz, he gave out the tricks of his trade and information on how the general public could spot his ex-partners in crime. (Despite his retirement, I think this move proved he still liked living dangerously.) First of all, here is his advice for anyone contemplating a life on the open road (with some more of my advice thrown in).

Tips for the Prospective Highwayman

1. Never stay in any one lodging (called a lubkin by the highwaymen) for any length of time and have a variety of false names at your command (that goes for writers as well).

2. In your lodgings, keep a selection of wigs, false beards, costumes, masks, and other disguises. When out robbing, put a pebble★ into your mouth to change the sound of your voice.

3. Have your own personal watchword or phrase, like "Got the time?" or "What shall we have for supper?" As soon as you say this, grab the victim's bridle and shove your pistol in his or her face (accompanied by a torrent of mean and nasty words). With a bit of luck, your victim should deliver the goods instantly (and be extremely confused).

4. If your victim's horse is faster, fresher, or prettier than yours, do not hesitate to exchange animals (or take both). But beware, someone could identify it later, so carry the means to disguise it (like something to color-in any white part).

5. Make your victim swear, on pain of a bullet in the brain, not to follow you or raise the alarm.

6. Always cut the girth and bridle of your victim's unstolen horse so that he can't chase after you.

7. When returning late from a night's work, muffle the sound of your horse's hooves by placing wool socks over them.

★*This is a tip for highwaymen and should not be tried at home.*

8.   If attacking a group, travel slowly on the road and let them catch up with you. Single out the one who looks the wealthiest and engage him or her in pleasant chitchat. If your victim doesn't know the fellow travelers, suggest that they're probably out to rob him. Once the two of you have fallen a few hundred yards behind the others, pull out your pistol and hold up your quarry.

8½.   Even better, hide some friends in the bushes waiting to hold up both of you. Snivel to your new friend and convince him that they will shoot you both if you don't deliver. Give the robbers (your friends) your money. Your new friend will almost certainly do the same. Finally, when your robbers gallop off, tell your fellow victim that you are sure you know which way the gang are going and point the other way.

9.   If you are ever caught and find yourself in court, have a story ready that will make the jurors weep with pity: impoverished family . . . dead parents . . . little brothers and sisters starving . . . stealing solely to feed them . . . ever so sorry . . . never do it again, etc.

10.   Why not try this? Arrive close to your proposed place of ambush, in a perfectly normal four-wheel open carriage with two horses. Change into your highwayman's outfit and unhitch one of the horses to ride during the robbery. When finished, reharness the horse to the perfectly normal carriage, change back into your normal clothes, and innocently drive home as if nothing happened.

11.   If the goods stolen are too recognizable to pawn in England, take them across the channel, especially to Holland where there's a ready market for diamonds and jewelry.

12.   Avoid mail coaches. They're too heavily armed, and you'll swing if you're caught.

Having said all this, many of the tricks of the trade mentioned above were frowned on by real "gentlemen of the road." They simply preferred to rely on a horse, a pistol, and a quiet road. Highwaymen were supposed to be "honest thieves" and would never use such low-down, common trickery. Right, and my name's Dick Turpin!

Tips for Seventeenth-Century Travelers

Jackson gave this advice to anyone contemplating taking valuables on a journey.

1. If you're carrying gelt (money), never tell anyone how much you have on you. Trust no one.

2. Never say when or where you're going, or good-bye, to anyone. Always try to slip away undetected.

3. Never travel on Sunday (the most dangerous day). The roads are quieter, and a highwayman stands less chance of being disturbed. Also, the county authorities will do nothing to help, as the Sunday Trading Act relieves them from the responsibility of reimbursing you if you get robbed.

4. Beware of any stranger who sidles alongside you and tries to chat. If someone does, keep changing pace, even to the point of stopping. If your new would-be pal follows suit, expect big trouble.

5. Try not to travel alone: there's safety in numbers.
6. Don't rely on the "silly, old decreeped men" (as Jackson described them) employed as watchmen at places where robberies have occurred. At any sign of trouble, they are more than likely to run (or hobble) as fast and as far away as possible.
7. Always say your prayers (and make your will) before setting off on a long journey.

Tips for Honest Innkeepers

The rare, respectable innkeepers acted as informants to the Bow Street Runners (early detectives in England, operating from Bow Street in London) and the thief-takers.

1. Keep a wary eye on anyone who seems too inquisitive about a fellow traveler—or about the traveler's horse, where he or she is going, or the intended time of departure.
2. Get the hostler (stableman) to examine a suspect's saddle bags to see whether they're empty. If they are, this means they're simply for show (and empty so that his horse can go that much faster).
3. When showing someone suspicious to a room, ask the servant to remain outside for a couple of seconds to listen for the jingling of coins. If the door's got a peephole—even better.
4. Get various people in your employ to ask a suspect's name. If he or she makes up a new name every day, the person will probably trip over his or her lies.
5. At dinnertime, tiptoe to the suspect's room and knock furiously at the door to announce that dinner is ready. Listen for scuffling, things falling over, or stuff being quickly stuffed away. Those noises mean the person is up to no good and trying quickly to hide it.

6. If your suspect's hanging around during the daytime and spots someone riding by who looks rich or has interesting baggage, see if your suspect jumps up and claims that the person is a beloved relation whom he (or she) simply must speak to—a sure sign.

Tips for Crooked Innkeepers

1. Tell your trusted staff to be alert for particularly heavy baggage. It probably contains coins.
2. Devise a way to get your hands on some of that money. This usually involves informing the highwayman with whom you're in cahoots so he can do the dirtier work.
3. Keep an eye out for money carriers, especially those transporting cash collected as taxes. Proceed to step two.

By the Way

On one occasion, a heavily escorted money carrier was robbed of a vast sum of tax money while traveling from Manchester to London. The thieves obviously weren't horse-lovers, as they stabbed to death sixteen of them, to prevent themselves from being followed.

CAUGHT GOOD AND PROPER

It's a sad fact, but most highwaymen spent their last days in prison. So what? you might think, prison life ain't so bad. Well, maybe not now (TVs in every cell, basketball games every afternoon, basic health care, etc.), but prisons in those days were rough, tough, miserable, horribly overcrowded, and no fun whatsoever. If you still had enough money, however, you could pay for a lot of the little comforts that made life bearable—but we'll go into that later.

The most infamous and most typical of all these prisons was called Newgate. The word alone sent shivers up the spine of anyone who'd done anything remotely bad in eighteenth-century London. It was first built on the site of the Old Bailey in 1218 and was only demolished (almost unbelievably) early in the twentieth century.

The Castle of Newgate (its nickname) was divided into three parts, one for men prisoners (that's where most of the highwaymen went), one for the ladies, and another for debtors (people who owed money).

By the Way

If a debtor was truly poor and had no hope of paying back his debt (and no fraud was involved), he could be let out. But, if the person to whom he owed money insisted, he could be kept in prison as long as that person paid the small cost of the debtor's weekly room and board.

Between these three sections were the keeper's house, lodgings for the turnkeys (the jailers), a chapel, a press room (coming later), condemned cells, and best of all, a taproom (bar), where jailers and visitors (or prisoners with money) could buy booze and fogus (tobacco). In an unofficial viewing gallery, the public could come and gawk at those poor souls condemned to death. The jailer charged an admission fee for this treat. For example, despite the unbelievable stench of the condemned hold, thousands of visitors in 1724 pressed vinegar-soaked hankies (bad enough, I think) to their noses and filed past the miserable highwayman Jack Shephard as he lay manacled and chained to the floor waiting to meet his end.

On the other hand, although chained up in their own private condemned cells, some wealthy highwaymen could still entertain visitors, right up until they were taken to Tyburn. William Hawkes, "the Flying Highwayman," visited with many lords and landed gentry in his cell. He managed to maintain a busy social schedule even in prison, continuing to charm friends with his ready wit until his execution in 1744.

By the Way

Some highwaymen, like Frenchman Claude Duval, became massive sex symbols to upper-class women—like rock or film stars. Many of the guys these ladies normally hung around (including the aristocracy) were unmanly to the point of effeminacy. The ladies swooned at the tales of the highwaymen's daring deeds.

No Go Area

But Newgate, through most of its history, was so filthy and disease ridden that even the rats thought twice about moving in. The atmosphere stank to high heaven, and visitors often fainted just breathing it in. Even the water, which came from a spring, met the overflow from the cesspool—a heady cocktail. Jail fever—the collective word for typhus, typhoid, and lots of other nastiness—did in more of the condemned than the actual gallows. The prisoners (albeit much like most of the population at the time) didn't receive even basic health care. Besides, doctors (nicknamed nim-glimmers) refused to go anywhere near the place. So did most other people, for that matter, as they soon turned into entertainment for the prisoners. The jailed tried to urinate or empty their chamber pots out of the windows onto the passersby. Residents of the underground women's quarters got a laugh by yelling nasty comments through gratings beside the pavement, thereby marring the public's view of the "feminine nature." All in all, Newgate was not somewhere you'd want to go for your vacation.

By the Way

The head keeper for each of the prisons paid a huge sum to get the job. As head of Newgate, for example, he would make a huge profit by charging fees of all the jailers, who would, in turn, extract cash from the prisoners.

Torture for All

The "press room" wasn't, as the name suggests, somewhere the local newspapers came to get the latest criminal gossip. It was a place for pressing confessions out of anyone whom the authorities thought was withholding information. They pressed highwaymen for information about their accomplices or where they'd stashed their loot. Jailers placed a heavily weighted (the equivalent of twenty-five large stones) door on the strapped-down "client's" chest. So far so bad. Then, after half an hour of this, one by one, extra weights were added until either:

a) the accused confessed (or lied just to get the weights off)
b) the victim died an excruciating death from a crushed chest—the air literally squeezed out of him.

This awful treatment wasn't abolished until 1792.

Newgate had all the normal old stuff, too, like whipping-blocks and the pillory. The pillory in those days revealed an interesting form of rough justice. A contraption like the old-fashioned village stocks and called a nutcracker by the highwaymen, the pillory held the prisoner in a standing position. This invited the general public to throw things at him (or her). If the mob didn't care much, they simply threw stuff like squashy fruit, old vegetables, and rotten eggs. Then it ended—they went home to a warm bath and bed. But if the public was really angry, they threw dead dogs and cats (and their respective muck), rocks, stones, or anything they could lay their hands on. It was not unknown for prisoners to be bludgeoned to death by this method.

By the Way

Sometimes the poor victim was nailed by his ear to the pillory and often had to leave the ear (and the other one) behind, when his time was up.

Some Newgate residents, who hadn't done anything bad enough to be hanged, were left to rot to death, manacled to their cell floors. With a little cash they could bribe their keepers into an "easement of irons," but this only lasted until the jailer decided the money had run out, kind of like a parking meter—well . . . kind of!

Not Bad

Despite all of this misery, at certain times in its history Newgate experienced a lighter side. In fact, in some respects

it became a fun place (but only if you had money). With only one jailer to ninety prisoners (one to six nowadays), the methods of discipline relaxed. The more crowded it got, the more impossible it became to keep track of everything and uphold some sense of order. For the right bribe, wives could stay overnight, children could live in, pets, pigs, and poultry could be kept (until 1792), and newspapers could be delivered. At one stage, a gymnasium area provided cramped prisoners a place to stretch their limbs. Sometimes, they threw wild and wicked parties, free from a lot of the restrictions that might have existed outside.

HOW TO HANG A HIGHWAYMAN

Strange as it might seem, hardly any of the better known highwaymen managed to avoid appearing before the law. If they weren't caught red-handed, many highwaymen ended up carelessly giving themselves away after they'd had too much to drink. Those who started bragging about their exploits down at the bar (as they often did) asked for trouble. As the old saying goes—walls have ears—even old walls (or old ears).

As for punishment, consider that in the seventeenth and eighteenth centuries the penalty for stealing a lace hankie or a spoon was exactly the same as for highway robbery or even murder. In fact, over 160 offenses could leave the culprit dangling on a rope. Theft of anything even modestly valuable carried the death sentence. Not much of a deterrent, if you think about it. If you were going to be hanged anyway, you might as well think big.

By the Way

Just in case you were considering going into the highway robbery business yourself, I have to warn you. It was quite common for kids at the age of thirteen—boys or girls—to be executed for the most petty of crimes (like not eating their peas). Having said that, it would probably be better for all concerned that you don't become highwaypeople at all (the last thing I need is an angry letter from your mom or dad).

Hanging on the Cheap

From the records of the *Western Flying Post*, 1812, comes the story of twenty-four-year-old James Williams, who jumped out on farmer Edward Locock while he was passing through the West Country. Williams forced Locock to hand over a handkerchief worth one shilling (about ten cents in today's U.S. money), a pair of gloves (also ten cents), the horse's bridle valued at four shillings (about thirty cents), his saddle at five shillings (about forty cents), an empty purse worth three pennies, and a couple of scraps of paper at only one penny— all in all no more than twelve shillings (about eighty-five cents). James was duly hanged at Exeter Gaol (jail) on Friday, April 18, 1812.

Hang 'em All

Hanging as a punishment for practically any social screw up got very out of hand. By the end of the eighteenth century, the judges decided to send everyone they possibly could to England's colonies instead (often a fate worse than death, in my opinion). They were dispatching more than a thousand people a year to rough, unwelcoming lands by the late 1700s.

This even applied to some highwaymen. If the prisoner had carried out his (or her) business without resorting to murder (violence was okay, but not murder), that person had a good chance of avoiding the rope at the gallows. (The highwaymen called the gallows the nubbing-cheat). Instead they took a nice long ocean cruise, usually to Maryland or Virginia or to the hot, sweaty plantations of the West Indies and later Australia. Not only that, but many a clever (for "clever" read "rich") prisoner could slip the judge a handful of gold coins to escape both. Despite this, more than 500 highwaymen's feet dangled above the ground (that's 250 highwaymen, by the way★) between 1750 and 1770. On one occasion, 40 highwaymen were hanged in one day.

★ *As long as there weren't any with only one leg.*

Hulks Ahoy

Before actually leaving England for their foreign visit, most highwaymen could expect to spend time on the disgusting, rotting hulks (a ship used as a prison). Those spooky, decommissioned ex-galleons stood on the wide part of the Thames River near London and at a few southern seaside ports.

In the 1700s, most of London's prisons were really only for people with money or for people waiting for their trial or for their execution. The reason for this was simple. Prisons in those days were nearly all privately owned, and debtors could be held there until they or their families coughed up the cash to get them out. In fact, in prisons like the infamous Newgate or Marshalsea, families often stayed together in cells the size of tiny (not to mention filthy) apartments. Imagine that! Your dad loses a bet down at the racetrack, and your entire family (dog included) has to go to prison with him. No fair!

Rich Pickings

Transportation to foreign parts of the world turned a profit for the shipowners who carried the convicts. They got between £10 and £25 (about $1,100 and $2,750 in modern

U.S. money) per person, if delivered alive and in one piece (not always the case), plus an extra £5 ($550) from the government back home. From 1788 onward, the powers that be decided that Australia might be a nice place to send convicts. Locked up in the filthy, sweaty holds of boats, the conditions were so awful on the eight-month voyages that many perished from various diseases before even reaching their destination. (Once there, many more perished from various new diseases.)

By the Way

Quite a few of the transported highwaymen, who tended to be smarter than the rest, escaped and set up business (robbing, of course) in their new country instead. The rest just tried to get home. Most of those who did get back to the old country, after serving their sentence, found themselves in exactly the same situation as they'd been before—broke! They simply got out their guns, saddled up their horses, slipped on their masks, and started again, as if nothing had happened.

Benefit of the Clergy

There used to be an effective trick called "Benefit of the Clergy" for getting out of the most serious sentences. Way back in the twelfth century, any person ordained (officially established) as a church official was entitled to trial in the church court rather than in the ordinary civil one. If found guilty under the jurisdiction of a bishop, he served a much lighter sentence (hanging wasn't allowed). Later on, this loophole opened to anyone who could prove ordination by taking a literacy test. (The clergy were usually the only ones who could read.) The accepted test for literacy was to be able to read the penitent's prayer (nicknamed the "neck verse"), which went:

Have Mercy on me, oh God
According to thy steadfast love;
According to thy abundant mercy
Blot out my transgressions.
Wash me thoroughly from my iniquity,
And cleanse me from my sin.

Well, playmates, it doesn't take the biggest genius who ever lived to figure out that anyone who could recite could easily cheat. On top of highwaymen being the better-educated felons, the illiterate guilty learned the verse parrot fashion (let's face it, have you ever heard of a parrot being hanged?). They could pass for clergy without being able to read at all. You'd think that someone would have attempted a pop quiz and presented a written Hail Mary or a Bible verse. Believe it or not, this stupid escape route was not totally abandoned until the 1800s.

Time to Be Hanged

Apart from London's famous hanging places, like Tyburn or Execution Dock in Wapping (for pirates) and, of course, prisons like Newgate, many were hanged or transported (when dead) to the very place where they'd committed the crime. As a warning to any people with similar ideas, they dangled from gibbets in sinister iron body-shaped cages. As their corpses gradually decomposed and their flesh rotted away to their bare bones, they inconsiderately created some of the most awful sights in history (next to my spaniel, Kevin). This treatment, by the way, was particularly popular if they'd robbed mail carriers. The foul practice went on until 1834.

Worse still was how some of the really creepy road robbers were gibbeted alive, hung up in the metal cages where they languished in agony, covered in flies, and pecked at by crows until dead. Anyone who tried to help them expected similar treatment. This happened to a few highwaymen who hung in agony (and with nothing to read) for days, until, if lucky, some kind passerby took a shot at him to put him out of his misery.

HOW ABOUT A TASTY HIGHWAYMAN?

Four Ways at Once

But that still was pretty mild stuff. Here's a story about what happened if they REALLY didn't like you. Let's examine the case of the highly educated and deeply refined Captain James Hind. This highwayman was a Royalist (a supporter of King Charles I during the English civil war). James specialized in robbing Roundheads (those against the king). As it turned out, he chose to rob the right side at the wrong time!

First of all, poor James was hanged by the neck for about five minutes (long enough to give him a severe sore throat, but not enough to kill him). As if that wasn't enough, he was then castrated (the cruelest cut of all), disembowelled, and saw his intestines burned in front of him—WHILE STILL ALIVE—OOOUUUCH! Finally he was beheaded (which usually does the trick), and his body was cut roughly (arms and legs attached) into four parts, doused in preserving fluid, and then sent to four different corners of the city wall.

Here's an account from some relatives who came to visit their recently executed family member:

"When we first came to Newgate there lay (in a little by-place like a closet near the room where we were lodged) the quartered bodies of three men that had been executed some days before. The heads were ordered to be set up in some part of the City. I saw the heads when they were brought up to be boiled . . . the Hangman put them into his kettle and parboiled them with bay salt and cummin seed [yum!], that to keep them from putrefaction and this to keep the fowls [birds] from seizing them."

By the Way

The idea of cutting someone into four parts, or removing any body parts, was based on the religious premise that in order to go to heaven your body must be in one piece (what about a saintly bishop with a wooden leg?). Oddly enough, this really used to worry the wigs off of even the most hardened criminals (I'd have thought he would have realized that he ruined his chances of a halo and wings long ago.)

Hanging for All

Let's get back to the actual hanging. As most highwaymen were kept in Newgate, we'll start there. On the prisoner's last night, the prison chaplain visited and tried to extract any further gory stories or confessions.

The canny old chaplains then sold the "account" to the local penny broadsheets (sensationalist newspapers like some of our tabloids). These papers were tossed to the crowds who lined the route to Tyburn or to the masses who gathered at the execution itself. The chaplains justified this blatant piece of profiteering by claiming that it showed the great masses how easy it was to graduate from little crimes to great big ones. Nice to see the clergy so in tune with their public, don't you think?

HOW TO HANG A HIGHWAYMAN

On hanging day, usually a Monday (and usually a public holiday, called Tyburn Fair Day), the condemned left by the back door of Newgate in a horse-drawn cart. Up to twenty people went at a time.

To remind the villains of their fate, they piled their coffins into the cart that followed the prisoners. Actually, the coffins were for the lucky ones. If there weren't enough coffins to go around, the others were gibbeted or dissected by eager medical students. In the carriage behind them rode the sheriffs of London just to make the occasion that much more special.

Famous highwaymen could attract up to 100,000 spectators, and, dressed in their finest clothes, they were generally cheered all along the procession's route. It was almost a happy occasion, like a royal wedding (if you think that's a happy occasion), with a bunch of street sellers providing anything from meat pies to sweets. It goes without saying that hanging days were like Christmas for pickpockets.

The procession soon passed the gates of Saint Sepulchre's Church on Newgate Street, where the condemned each received a little bunch of flowers before traveling along the Tyburn Valley. Then they went onward up Heavy (now Holborn) Hill and through the Holborn tollgate, which marked the boundary of London. (The little group was now, believe it or not, in the countryside.) They then traveled along Holborn, Saint Giles, and around nasty marshland. At the halfway mark, the occupants were allowed a last drink (Perrier, naturellement) at a tavern called The Bowl. The little procession then progressed along Oxford Street to Tyburn Tree (modern Marble Arch). All in all, they traveled a distance of only three miles, but it often took up to two hours.

Time to Talk

On reaching the gallows, the more famous highwaymen were allowed to give a good-bye speech—sometimes lasting up to an hour and often really funny. The crowd loved this part and booed if the victim showed any sign of fear. Some felons attacked the actual hangman, or even the chaplain, and the crowd loved such demonstrations.

The Bitter End

Very often, as a perk of the job, the hangman (whom the highwaymen called the nubbing-cove) was allowed to keep the deceased's clothes to wear or to sell to the crowd. As the body was taken down from the scaffold, the crowd surged forward to touch it or to try to remove some little memento. It was thought that the "death sweat" of a recently executed person (especially of a highwayman) contained magical medical powers. A sick mother, for example, fought to brush the limp hand against her face or the faces of her kids. If a woman could not have children, the magic hand was thought to reverse it. If you were lucky enough to be given the skull, it could be used as a cup. A person who drank from the cup could be cured of epilepsy. If said skull was left long enough to gather mold or moss, the scrapings were supposed to cure headaches (beats aspirin, I suppose). One beautiful woman was seen to expose her breast in front of thousands of cheering onlookers and place the dead hand upon it. Aren't some people weird?

Almost best of all (if you're as gruesome as me)—if a hanged man's hand fell into the possession of burglars, they dried and pickled it and used it as a candleholder. Instead of candles the actual fingers could be lit. Why bother? Because, if the burglar entered a house carrying this weird candelabra, it was thought that the poor occupants would fall under a  spell. Then the burglars could do their work in peace. With all of these valuable souvenirs to be had, it's no wonder people of the time called Tyburn the Paddington Fair. It was just a carnival full of prizes for everyone but the highwaymen.

THIEF-TAKERS

Before I tell you who and what thief-takers were, it might be necessary to drone on about how the law in England was (or wasn't) enforced all those years ago. Right up to the late 1700s, any real grown-up, organized form of law and order in England was resisted by the rich and powerful as they claimed (quite rightly) that it would interfere with liberty. What they really meant was that, as they were so corrupt themselves, any form of law and order would definitely interfere with their liberty to continue the questionable dealings that they'd been getting away with for years.

To fight crime, there were local constables (amateurs), night-watchmen (called Charlies), and beadles (local church officials) in London. They were, however, well aware that they were unable to do much to stop the enormous surge of crime. The constables, for instance, were simply ordinary members of the public who, when their name came up, had to do a year's service for no money—a dangerous and thankless task (like writing these books!). Most times, these good men of London did their level best to get out of it, even paying others, if at all possible, to do their duty for them.

By the Way

There used to be something called the "Tyburn ticket" in the eighteenth century: a system by which any constable, if he managed to get someone convicted and hung at the famous gallows (Tyburn), could be let off the rest of his term.

Thief-Takers

Thief-taking started in the late 1600s, during the reign of William and Mary. Some clever folks decided that the answer to all the robbery on the public thoroughfares was to set up a system of rewards. They offered them to anyone who could supply information that would lead to the arrest of a highwayman (in particular) or any number of other criminals. In other words, a tattletale's reward was exemption from crimes he'd committed.

How Much?

In the beginning, the bounty for a highwayman was £40 ($4,400)—plus, would you believe, the highwayman's money, weapons, and even his horse. (I suppose where he was going, he wouldn't need any of those.) So far so good, I expect you think. Trust me, it all went a bit crazy. The powers-that-be also offered a free pardon to the tattletale. Anyone who was either convicted of a crime or about to be was let off. Now, it doesn't take Sherlock Holmes to figure this one out. If you were, how shall I put it, not very honest and had a lot of not-very-honest friends, you could make yourself a good business out of snitching on them and copping the reward. The professional thief-taker or bounty hunter was born.

It was a good system but seriously open to corruption. Just think, a private individual would not only put the word out if he or she had been robbed but would even employ other private individuals to track down the culprit. For this, the

"detective" would get about half of everything he managed to retrieve. Plus he received a large fee for bringing the criminal to justice. So far so good—but have you spotted the other potential scam? If you were really clever and really, really tricky, you could actually organize the robberies, contact the victim, return the stolen goods, and then, here's the good part, turn in the guys you got to do it, for yet another reward—three sources of cash in one. Wicked admittedly, but nonetheless brilliant.

On June 3, 1752, a professional thief-taker, Thomas Norton, took a coach to Halfway House, a stop between Knightsbridge and Kensington in London. He had heard a tip-off that the house was going to be robbed. Sure enough, the famous highwayman William Belcher showed up and was arrested by Norton as they each went about their business.

Jonathan Wild

Best, or should I say worst, of the bunch of thief-takers was a guy called Jonathan Wild, who, on the surface, seemed like a highly respectable London magistrate. Underneath he turned out to be a lying, cheating scoundrel. First of all, he planned brilliant robberies for thieves and highwaymen throughout the land, mostly using men who'd illegally escaped from hard labor in England's overseas colonies. He then received anything they stole and tried to sell it back to the original owners. If the thieves refused to play or even complained, he turned them in. That meant, when it came right down to it, they were being blackmailed. The men he did inform on were almost always found guilty. All in all,

JONATHAN WILD

Wild, later nicknamed the "Thief-Taker General of Great Britain and Ireland," managed to send over sixty criminals to their deaths on the gallows and picked up a tidy pocketful of blood money (which is where the term came from).

Because of the number of crooks he sent to the gallows, Wild tried (albeit unsuccessfully) to become a Freeman of the City of London (a big deal in the olden days). He strutted around the streets, silver-topped cane in hand, as if he owned the place. For several years, highwaymen avoided London like the plague.

I suppose, that in a funny sort of roundabout way, he actually did succeed in ridding the city of a well-known scourge. Eventually, however, Jonathan Wild took a tumble over a little piece of French lace that one of his robbers had stolen, and he (Wild) had tried to wheedle a reward from. Not much in itself, but the link that everyone suspected was made, and it was all the authorities needed to slap him in jail and eventually string him up. His execution, when still only forty-three, prompted a frenzied response from the public whom he had so cynically betrayed. He was spat at and booed all the way to the gallows.

THE BEGINNING OF
THE END

Henry Fielding was the famous novelist and playwright who wrote the rather rude (but funny) book *Tom Jones* and was, to most people, an all-around good egg. He was made a magistrate in Westminster (part of London) and moved into the area of Bow Street in central London to run his office from home. To tell the truth, the reason he took the job was not for any do-gooding motive. He was short of ready cash. But old Henry had been casually observing the rapid rise in robbery for years. He had noticed how the private thief-takers had got a stranglehold on the capturing and rewarding side of the business. Sure, said Henry, you could continue upping the rewards for the arrest of villains, but that would simply be doling out cash to those thieving thief-takers. (These guys were even up to tempting innocent youngsters to commit crimes simply so they could arrest them and pocket the rewards.)

Fielding also despaired about the decrepit Charlies, the rickety old watchmen, not to mention the unpaid constables, who were only really interested in passing the job on to some other poor sucker. As for executions or public hangings, he decided that, although they weren't that fun for the highwaymen (even though they mostly seemed to make a joke of it), the events had simply become a fabulous day out for all the family—an entertainment for the masses—a theme park with hanging (and worse) as the main attraction. Despite the number of necks the authorities stretched, they seemed to be going nowhere toward scaring off others. He was well aware that a huge number of poor folks went rumbling past his place in the tumbrels on their merry way to Tyburn and death. He knew they were few in comparison to the hundreds of others that were *not* (and who should have been).

Fielding decided that the only answer was to make the actual doing of the crimes less easy, and the only way to do that was to start a police force (even if he didn't know what the words meant). Old Fielding scoffed at those who said it would take away English freedoms. He assured them, quite rightly, that they'd only lose their freedom if they actually did something wrong.

The first step was to get the pawnbrokers (the legal receivers of secondhand goods) on his side. He asked them nicely to check the lists of stolen items and report anything suspicious that was offered to them. Fielding then put an ad in the papers (or penny broadsheets) offering to interview anyone who'd been robbed. Would you believe that nobody had ever thought of that before?

Mr. Fielding's People

Fielding met a guy named Welch who'd been made head of the Holborn nonpaid constables and was apparently an honest man (rare in those days). Together they formed the first criminal investigation unit, using six of Welch's most trustworthy constables as investigators. Still no pay involved for these guys, but they could receive decent rewards for anyone they caught.

But if you ever think modern London must be less safe than ever before, think again. It was a nightmare (literally) for the nighttime traveler in 1750. Highwaymen or footpads lurked in practically every shadow and behind every tree. As Horace Walpole, another famous writer, wrote, "Robbing is the only thing that goes on with any vivacity," and that "going to a friend's house in London is as dangerous as going to the relief of Gibraltar."★ On another occasion, he said, "one is forced to travel even at noon as if one is going to battle." It has to be said that no crime wave in history even remotely compared to the one in England in the mid-eighteenth century. And, if you don't believe me, even the king was held up by a highwayman in his own backyard at Kensington Palace!

Anyway, these slightly wet-behind-the-ears policemen, nicknamed Mr. Fielding's People, did well at first. However, their successes were still a drop in the ocean compared to all the stuff that was still going on. Too many highwaymen got away scot-free. If something wasn't done soon, Fielding ranted, every street in London and all the roads leading to it and from it would be impassable—and impossible.

But by now Henry was old, sick, and in a wheelchair. So he asked the government if his half-brother John could share the job with him. A fine pair they made: Henry was dying and his half-brother (to be nicknamed the "Blind Beak") was blind (not even half-blind). John must have looked fairly menacing

★ *Big news story of the time. In 1704, during the War of the Spanish Succession, Gibraltar was captured by English and Dutch forces.*

when suspects appeared before him in court as he wore a black strip of cloth around his sightless eyes.

By the Way

Blind John's hearing was so sharpened by his blindness that it was alleged that he could distinguish the voices of over three thousand different thieves.

A Proper Plan

The minister in charge of crime and that sort of thing, the duke of Newcastle, not only agreed with the Fieldings' concern but asked the two brothers to draw up a suitable plan to solve it. The first thing they did was to turn Henry's house into a twenty-four-hour manned police station. Amazingly, it still is a station, although the present building (built in 1879) is on the other side of the road. The Fieldings then organized to have two men always on call (and on horses) and to keep a list of all the crimes that had occurred and of all the people that just might have done them. Then, as now, it was usually just a case of pairing them up. All in all, it cost £600 ($66,000) a year to run the operation, which was a lot of money in those days. But, compared to the amount of rewards that they dished out to those pesky thief-takers, it was peanuts.

Bow Street Runners

Unfortunately, the Bow Street Runners, as they were officially called, were viewed at first in exactly the same light as the thief-takers by the general public. But no one could deny the success they were beginning to have (the number of big crimes in London dropped like a stone). There was still a long way to go, however, because highway robberies outside the city were almost as bad as ever. John Fielding decided that the general public wasn't on the ball enough. In 1755 he issued a

BOW STREET RUNNER

"Plan for Preventing Robberies within Twenty Miles of London." In the plan, he begged the public to help in any way they knew how and to let his guys know of crimes as soon as they happened.

Costly Business

Poor John had more things to worry about. The British government was slow in paying him back the money he dished out to pursue highwaymen. It was an expensive business to be sure.

Things continued to get worse. So in 1761 John put forward another far-reaching plan. The government rejected most of it, admittedly, but agreed to fund a civilian horse patrol of ten men (and presumably ten horses)—five experienced, five not. The effects were immediate. By the spring of 1764, all the roads leading out of London had been made safe. Too safe! The government, seeing the problem was practically over, decided to abandon the horse patrol. And guess what? Within a few weeks, those wily old robbers were all back and at it again.

Back Again

The government reluctantly coughed up again, and again the highwaymen hightailed it back to where they came from. Unbelievably, shortly after, the horse patrol was abandoned again—and this time for ages. By the 1770s, the roads were worse than ever before, with just about everyone, lord or lout, lady or lass, being held up on the roads leaving London as a matter of course—of course!

By the Way

London had to wait until 1805 for a regular horse patrol to be reinstated. That marked the beginning of a rather swift end for the highwaymen of England.

THE BEST OF THE BUNCH

Claude Duval—The Most Charming

A miller's son, Claude Duval was born in France (Normandy to be precise) in 1643. When a teenager, he moved to Paris where he met lots of Royalist Englishmen on the run from the civil war. Claude came to England as a servant to the duke of Richmond (it was popular in those days to have French staff). Being an adventurous guy, he found this job boring and decided on a career of robbing people. He must have been very good, because he had reached the top of the wanted list (the highwaymen's hit parade) by 1668.

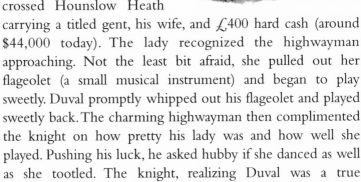

OF COURSE WE WERE ROBBED BY CLAUDE DUVAL

Claude Duval gained a massive reputation with the general public, especially the ladies. He was handsome, witty, and terribly flirtatious (with a French accent). He was *so* popular with his female fans, in fact, that it became quite a status symbol to get yourself held up by him.

On one occasion, a coach crossed Hounslow Heath carrying a titled gent, his wife, and £400 hard cash (around $44,000 today). The lady recognized the highwayman approaching. Not the least bit afraid, she pulled out her flageolet (a small musical instrument) and began to play sweetly. Duval promptly whipped out his flageolet and played sweetly back. The charming highwayman then complimented the knight on how pretty his lady was and how well she played. Pushing his luck, he asked hubby if she danced as well as she tootled. The knight, realizing Duval was a true gentleman (who had a huge pistol in his hand), allowed the lady to dance with the robber in the moonlight. Duval, of course, danced beautifully and returned the lady flushed and swooning to her carriage.

He then casually reminded the knight that the purpose of the meeting was cash—his cash! "I'll tell you what," he laughed, "why not regard it as payment for the entertainment." The knight found this suggestion reasonable and was handing over the £400 when Duval said he would only take £100 because of his wife's charming performance.

Duval was eventually picked up, armed to the teeth and drunk as a skunk, in a tavern in London. He was sentenced to death. Though countless well-connected people tried desperately to get him off, he was hanged at Tyburn in 1670 when still only twenty-seven years of age.

The poor ex-highwayman was taken to lie "in state" at the notorious Tangier Tavern in London. It is no exaggeration to say that a procession of upscale dames wearing masks (so as not to be recognized) stopped to weep over his body. It was surrounded by candles and watched over by eight tall men in black cloaks—to prevent the ladies from throwing themselves on the corpse. This poem was later engraved on his gravestone:

Here lies Du Vall; Reader, if Male thou art,
Look to thy purse; if Female, to thy heart.
Much havoc has he made of both; for all
Men he made stand, and women he made fall.
The second Conqueror of the Norman race,★
Knights to his arms did yield, and Ladies to his face.
Old Tyburn's glory; England's illustrious thief,
Du Vall, the Ladies' joy; Du Vall, the Ladies' grief.

★ *William was the first.*

Dick Turpin—The Most Notorious

Just mention highwaymen, and everyone thinks of Dick Turpin. He's generally thought of as a brave, romantic, swashbuckling figure much like Robin Hood. But, like Robin Hood (who probably didn't even exist), a lot of the stories are exaggerated and even blatant lies. For instance, he never had a horse called Black Bess and never did that famous ride from London to York in one go—so there!

In fact, instead of being the gallant, handsome gentleman of the road, it is reported that he was exceedingly cruel and ugly to boot. Mean and ugly okay, but brave nonetheless. The "King of the Road," as he was nicknamed, was born in 1706 in Essex, southeastern England, the son of an innkeeper. He started his working life as a trainee butcher in London. While running his own shop, he discovered that there was much more money to be made from stealing the animals that he was to chop up and sell. But he was soon found out and had to get out of town and back to Essex pretty quickly.

We next hear of him as a smuggler in Canvey Island, Essex—well, not actually a smuggler, but someone who cunningly held up smugglers after they'd done all the hard work. Turpin did this by pretending to be a revenue officer, but again was soon found out and had once more to scurry away. It was then on to deer rustling with the infamous Essex Gang, who supplemented their income with a little local housebreaking.

The Essex Gang was a mean bunch to be sure, robbing throughout the Epping Forest area. Soon there was a huge reward on each of their heads. But Dick got fed up with group crime and wanted to go it alone. He did, in 1735, when he started out as a solo highwayman at the age of twenty-nine. Within two years, he was by far the most famous robber throughout the length and breadth of England and almost a folk hero in his native Essex.

Later, by the way, he specialized in the public land between Barnes and Wandsworth in London (now the common haunt of dastardly estate agents and cowboy builders). He was easily recognizable for his pale, pockmarked, broad face and intense, staring eyes.

Dick teamed up for a while with a fellow robber named Tom King. They lived (some of the time with Mrs. Turpin) in a cave in the middle of the Epping Forest. There they could hide for weeks on end, even though they had their horses with them. They were close to two roads (which they watched through peepholes, always scouting potential victims).

What made Turpin famous was his staggering brutality, which was unusual among the elite of the profession. Unlike his fellow highwaymen, he had no problem with hurting and killing. Sure, most highwaymen threatened—but few actually did what they said they were going to do. Dick's reasoning was simple, however. He must have thought, if I'm going to get hanged for robbery anyway, I might as well get rid of the witnesses. It sort of worked. For ages he remained free—nobody dared to risk collecting the reward for telling on him.

His first murder victim was one of the forest keepers who followed him to his secret hole. The next was his own partner, Tom King, whom he shot accidentally (whoops!) while aiming at a Bow Street Runner who'd recognized them. (Pistols in those days left a lot to be desired accuracy-wise.) In a weird fit of revenge for the tragic mistake (which was nobody's fault but his own), Turpin went on a spree of robbing. He held up someone every single day for the next month or so.★

THAT'S SIX TIMES THIS WEEK!

Turpin eventually turned his back on highway robbery when the amount of money on his head reached £200 (about $22,000 in today's money). But Dick simply couldn't go straight. A year later, he was caught, accused of horse-stealing, and sentenced to hang.

Dick Turpin, by the way, was very jolly and sociable while waiting in prison for his big day. He was convinced it would never happen. But happen it did—in York on April 7, 1739. The most famous of all highwaymen died bravely, confessing in the end to countless robberies and apologizing only for killing the man who'd stumbled on his hideout in the forest. He then chucked himself into the air with a chuckle and died dangling five minutes later. He was only thirty-three years old.

★ *It was someone different every day, by the way, otherwise the person would have got very bored with it.*

By the Way

If you want to see Dick's prison cell, visit the Castle Museum in York.

John Cottington —The Bravest

John Cottington (alias "Mulled Sack" after his favorite drink) had a difficult start in life. His dad, a hatmaker, died a hopeless drunk, leaving little John, his mother, and his eighteen brothers and sisters destitute (not much time for hatmaking). John's first real job was working for five women in the head-shaving business (wigs were so sweaty).

That job ended when they were all sent to the pillory or deported for various petty crimes. So from an early age, the lad was out on the streets stealing anything that might be turned into money to buy food.

A true Londoner, and yet another staunch follower of the king, John carefully chose those he robbed and never touched anyone loyal to the royals. Having been at it since childhood, he became a pro, even carrying chain-cutting scissors (specially made for him) to sever necklaces, watch-chains, bracelets, and purses from their unsuspecting owners. One of his most famous prey was Oliver Cromwell, leader of the Roundheads in the civil war. That was about the worst career move John could make—it nearly got him hanged.

After this incident, he decided to pack up the small stuff and become a real highwayman, choosing Hounslow Heath as his area of operations. He teamed up with an ex-soldier, Tom Cheyney. Cheyney was hurt seriously in a holdup that went wrong. They bravely, if somewhat stupidly, took on a whole troop of soldiers. So seriously hurt was Tom, in fact, that the powers that be had to hurry through his trial and execution in case he died first. Poor Tom was found guilty at lunchtime and hanged only a few hours later that afternoon, probably a Guinness world record.

"Mulled Sack" went on to become one of the most successful highwaymen of all time. He once robbed a heavily protected army pay-wagon of £4,000 (about $440,000 these days) in hard cash. Be that as it may, he, just like his partner, was caught and hanged in 1656—still a relatively young man.

Lady Katherine Ferrers—the Prettiest

Lady Katherine Ferrers, like her male counterparts in the highway-robbery business, came from the other side of society—the top drawer in fact. At sixteen, she had married the extremely rich Lord Ferrers. She was a beautiful and dutiful wife in their massive mansion just outside of London.

One day, she decided her life was too tedious and boring. Unfortunately, most society women didn't have jobs, nor could they hang out at coffee shops or shopping malls. So Lady Katherine had to find something else constructive to do with her time. Kathy waited until the end of the evening and kissed her old hubby goodnight (they often had separate bedrooms in those days). She dressed up in her hidden highwayman's outfit, took a secret passage out of the house, and robbed coaches as they came and went from the city. Obviously Mrs. Ferrers wasn't in it for the money—simply for the buzz.

Lady Katherine did this until eventually she was wounded in a shoot-out during a holdup. Legend has it, she bled to death halfway up the stairs, having staggered all the way home.

(A good argument for one-floor homes, I'd have said.) She was still only twenty-two years old, poor dear.

Zachary Howard—the Boldest

Yet another Royalist highwayman was Captain Zachary Howard. He was so loyal to Charles I that he mortgaged his extremely valuable property in Wales to raise an army to fight for him. When the king lost his head, Zachary lost his home and lands and sailed to France. He returned to Scotland with Charles I's kid, Charles II, who was trying to get his dad's country back. Unfortunately, with a lot of money offered for Zach's capture, by then the only real future for him was as a highwayman. It must be said in his defense, however, that he only robbed those who were politically opposed to the king.

His jaunts went down in history for their daring and downright barefaced nerve. On one occasion, he halted a well-known Roundhead who was traveling with a servant. Highwayman Howard was told in no uncertain terms to go away, but he promptly robbed his victim of a diamond ring and all of his gold. Bursting with laughter, he then set the gentleman on his servant's horse facing its backside and tied the servant to his master, facing the horse's head. A sharp slap on the beast's rump, and it was in this predicament that master and servant eventually trotted into the next town.

Before long there was the unheard-of reward of £500 ($55,000) for Zachary Howard's head. Undeterred, the brave captain decided after a short "rest" in Ireland to take his best shot at his worst enemy, Oliver Cromwell. So saying, he contrived to stay (in disguise) at the same inn in northwestern England as the big boss himself. The story goes that Howard soon made friends with the rebel leader and was invited to his room for prayers. He promptly pulled out his pistol, tied old Ollie up, took all his money, and, as an afterthought, picked up the nearly full chamber pot (no bathrooms in those days) and crowned Cromwell "in the manner he deserved."

Like so many good stories, there's a sad end to this one. When Howard was eventually caught in 1652, the still-furious Cromwell came to see him at Maidstone Gaol (jail) and personally saw to his execution.

William Davis—the Most Devious

Wealthy farmer, pillar of respectable society, regular churchgoer, father of eighteen kids—these aren't qualities you instantly connect with a life of robbery on the open road. But William Davis (the Golden Farmer) was all of these things. He got away with part-time robbery for more than forty years, even in broad daylight, by his mastery of the art of disguise. Many of William's victims, usually cattlemen on their way home from the market with gold coins jingling in their pockets, were men who knew him pretty well in everyday life.

On one occasion, after his landlord visited and collected his annual rent, William donned a disguise and followed him up the road. The landlord, not knowing him from Adam, claimed, on being held up, that he only had a few pence on him. Davis knew better and took his rent money back.

When he was eventually shot and captured, the whole neighborhood was in an uproar. He was someone they had all looked up to. And look up to him they still did, for his body, after being hanged, was left to rot in chains and shackles (called darbies by highwaymen) in Surrey, near where he'd farmed for years.

THE END OF THE ROAD

By the end of the eighteenth century, things were getting pretty tough for the average hardworking highwayman. For a start, for some time he'd had to contend with the reward system, whereby any little underworld sneak could whisper a name to any Bow Street Runner or thief-taker and make a nice little pile of money.

There was also the onset of better roads. This meant that coaches seldom went as slow or broke down as often. Sometimes they even charged past the poor chilly highwayman who'd been hanging out for ages.

Better roads also meant more traffic, which, instead of providing more business, actually annoyed highwaymen a lot. Robbing defenseless coaches depended on the roads being deserted. I mean, imagine being a highwayman these days. You'd have to do all your robbing at gas stations.

On top of all that, the poor guys had to contend with all those tollhouse keepers, who were beginning to get friendly with the Bow Street Runners, passing on information gleaned from the travelers. The net was tightening like a . . . tight net!

Don't Fence Me In

But worse still was the dratted enclosure system, which stitched up England. Instead of the wide open spaces to escape over, highwaymen had to run in and out and around a labyrinth of hedges and fences enclosing smaller and smaller fields. Hardly any horses, by the way, had been taught to jump over things in those days.* So, the poor old highwayman, if

---

★ *At least that meant they didn't have to put up with show jumping.*

cornered, found himself having to get off and walk his horsey around the obstacle if he wanted to escape.

No Room at the Inn

The highwayman was becoming a social leper. Even finding somewhere to rest for the night and to have a drink and something to eat (and pore over the loot) was becoming tricky. There were fewer and fewer licences dished out to landlords who were known to offer highwaymen hospitality (and the knowing wink).

Nothing to Steal

But difficult as all of this was, he still worked on the assumption that there was something out there on the open roads yet to steal. This wasn't always true. No one "bled freely," as the highwaymen said about those who got robbed easily, anymore. It had taken a long time, but the early banks had eventually grasped that huge amounts of cash had been lost by their clients, especially animal traders, on their way home from the London markets. They started a system by which the cash could be paid into accounts in the City (London's financial district)—the beginning of modern banking. Eventually, even the deals themselves were done with notes of credit (early checks), which was all terrible news for the poor, patient highwayman waiting in the shadows for cash on delivery.

The gradual establishment of banks really put the kibosh on things. By the end of the eighteenth century, it was mostly boring old checks and bills of sale being carried in place of the wonderfully untraceable silver and gold (called "yellow boy" by the highwaymen, for some reason). Checks, as you might imagine, weren't much use if you didn't have a bank account—and highwaymen generally didn't.

Blood Money for All

When the general public got in on the act and realized that they could receive rewards for informing on highwaymen, the end finally loomed into view. Suddenly our poor hero found himself with no friends, nowhere to rob, nothing to steal, and nowhere to go (after not having done anything). By the late 1700s, it was more or less all over.

HIGHWAYMAN SPEAK

Adam's ale: water (still in use)

autem-mort: a married woman

back'd: dead

bandittis: highwaymen

belly-cheat: an apron

bene-cove: a good man

bene-darkmans: good night

bilk the rattling cove: to cheat a coachman (bilk is still used by cab drivers)

binged awast in the darkness: fled by night

bingo: brandy

bingo-boy: a lover of strong drink

bit: to thieve

bite the bill from the cull: steal a sword from a gentleman's side

bite the biter: rob another thief

black-spy: a real nasty guy

bleed freely: easily robbed

bluffer: an innkeeper

caffin: cheese

darbies: prison fetter, handcuffs, or shackles (still in use)

darkmans: the night

dim mort: a babe

duds: clothes (still in use)

earnes: share of the loot

equipped: rich

fencing-cully: a receiver of stolen goods

fogus: tobacco

gelt: money (still in use)

gentry-cove: a gentleman

gentry-mort: a gentlewoman

glaziers: eyes

grinders: teeth

hamlet: a high constable

hick: a rather thick country man (still in use)

joseph: a coat (maybe from Joseph's coat of many colors)

kicks: pants

kinchen: children

knight of the road: a talented highwayman

lobkin: a lodging house

lowpad: the lowest form of thief

lurries: easily removable jewelry

moon-curser: someone who robs only by moonlight

nab: a hat

nim-glimmer: a doctor or surgeon

nubbing-cheat: the gallows

nubbing-cove: a hangman

nubbing-ken: a court or place for a trial

nutcracker: the pillory

ogles: eyes (still in use)

Paddington Fair: Tyburn

prance: a horse

rattler: a coach

rattler-cove: a coachman

rum-ogles: charming eyes (referring to women)

sack: a pocket

shappo (from the French *chapeau*): a very expensive hat

squeek: a victim yelling for help

tatler: a watch

tip: to help a comrade in trouble

togemans: a cloak or coat

velvet: a tongue

whiddle: one who talks too much and gives away secrets

xantippe: a nagging woman

yarum: milk

yellow boy: gold

FURTHER READING

Ash, Russell. *Discovering Highwaymen*. Buckingham, England: Shire Publications, 1999.

Billet, Michael. *Highwaymen and Outlaws*. London: Arms and Armour, 1997.

Blackwood, Gary L. *Highwaymen*. Tarrytown, NY: Benchmark Books, 2001.

Brandon, David. *Stand and Deliver!* Gloucester, England: Sutton Publishing, 2001. (for older readers)

Dickens, Charles. *Oliver Twist*. New York: Random House Children's, 1994.

Dunford, Stephen. *The Irish Highwaymen*. Dublin: Merlin Publishing, 2001.

Finger, Charles J. *Highwaymen*. New York: RM McBride & Company, 1923.

Garfield, Leon. *Smith*. New York: Farrar, Straus and Giroux, 2000.

Howson, Gerald. *Thief-Taker General*. Somerset, NJ: Transaction Publishers, 1985.

Kerr, Daisy. *Bandits*. New York: Franklin Watts, 1998.

Lawrence, Iain. *The Smugglers*. New York: Delacorte Press, 1999.

Noyes, Alfred. *Highwayman*. New York: William Morrow, 1983.

Waller, Maureen. *1700: Scenes from London Life*. New York: Four Walls Eight Windows, 2000. (for older readers)

WEBSITES

The Bushranger Site (Highwaymen in Australia)
   <http://scs.une.edu.au/bushrangers/home.htm>
Cavaliers and Cut-Throats
   <http://members.aol.com/maddy28/hmyth/highway.htm>
Dick Turpin
   <http://www.britannia.com/BritHeritage/turpin.html>
Famous Highwaymen
   <http://www.contemplator.com/history/famous.html>
The Highwaymen Ghosts
   <http://www.mysterymag.com/html/highwayman.html>
Highwaymen in the 17th and 18th Century
   <http://www.historic-uk.com/HistoryUK/England-
   History/Highwaymen.htm>
Highwaymen, Rogues, and Brigands
   <http://loggerheads.biz/history_crime.htm>
Outlaws and Highwaymen
   <http://www.outlawsandhighwaymen.com/>
Prisoners of Newgate
   <http://www.exclassics.org/newgate/>
Public Execution in Early Modern England
   <http://www.unc.edu/~charliem/index.htm>

INDEX

ABOUT THE AUTHOR

John Farman has worked as a commercial illustrator and a cartoonist and has written more than thirty nonfiction books for children. He lives in London, England.